The Urgency of Snails

Also by Robin Gilbert

Poetry:
My Own Dragon (Caro Publishing, 2006).
DaDa & the Dark Lady (Shepton Dragon, 2012 – reprinted with corrections 2013).

Other:
'The Taylor Family of Ongar and Their Houses There' in *Aspects of the History of Ongar*, ed. Michael Leach (1999). pp.50–103.
Articles in the *Oxford Dictionary of National Biography* (2004) on Joseph Gilbert (1732–1820), Isaac Taylor (1730–1807), Charles Taylor (1756–1823), Isaac Taylor (1759–1829), Mrs Ann Taylor (1757–1830), Jefferys Taylor (1792–1853).
Those Who Served – Casualties of the Great War in a Corner of Gloucestershire (Shepton Dragon, 2015).

Edited by Robin Gilbert:
The Poetry of P. A. T. O'Donnell (Shepton Dragon, 2010).
Prospero's Trilby – the Youthful Poems 1994–1999 of Sam Gilbert (Shepton Dragon, 2011).
Dear World – a Cheltenham Poetry Festival anthology of poems on the environment (Frosted Fire Press, 2015).

THE URGENCY OF SNAILS

ROBIN GILBERT

Graffiti Books

The Urgency of Snails
Robin Gilbert

Published by Graffiti Books, 2025
Malvern, Worcestershire, United Kingdom
Email: graffitibooksuk@gmail.com
Website: www.graffitibooks.uk

Graffiti Books is the book publishing arm of *Graffiti Magazine*

Designed, printed and bound by Aspect Design
89 Newtown Road, Malvern, Worcs. WR14 1PD
United Kingdom
Tel: 01684 561567
E-mail: allan@aspect-design.net
Website: www.aspect-design.net

All Rights Reserved.

Copyright © 2025 Robin Gilbert

Robin Gilbert has asserted his moral right
to be identified as the author of this work.

The right of Robin Gilbert to be identified as the author
of this work has been asserted in accordance with
Section 77 of the Copyright, Designs and Patents Act 1988.

This book is sold subject to the condition that it shall not, by way of trade or otherwise, be lent, resold, hired out or otherwise circulated without the publisher's prior consent in any form of binding or cover other than that in which it is published and without a similar condition including this condition being imposed on the subsequent purchaser.

Cover image Copyright © 2025 Robin Gilbert

ISBN 978-1-0684883-0-6

*This collection is dedicated to the memory of
three special people and poets I have been privileged to know:
Michael Newman, Marianne Hellwig John, Ann Drysdale*

Contents

November	1
Lineover Wood*	3
In Witcombe Wood	4
Mussel shell	5
Shells	6
Drought*	7
Damp humours	8
Peter Grimes	10
After the rain	11
In the flooded lane	11
In winter	12
Branches	12
Spider threads	13
Keys to a kingdom	14
Last fruit	15
Ivy	16
Halcyon wars	18
Sparrowhawk	20
Swifts*	21
Aerobatics	21
The Magpie with a broken wing	22
Bumbarrel Valentine*	24
Heron	26
Welcome home	27
The last passenger pigeon	28
Birds*	29
Pecking orders*	30
Old friend	32
Grass snake	34
Sloth	35
Monkey sanctuary	36

Pigs	37
In a small way	38
Cornish miracle	39
In a time of prayer	40
Glass	42
Has it come to this?	43
The pool	44
Dark Lane*	46
Dee	48
Beeching	50
Night walk at Stowe	52
Anchor Island	54
Earth	56
Schrödinger's mole	57
The Wild Hunt	58
Primaeval	59
Pax Romana	60
King Lear on Crickley Hill	62
Eutopia	63
The ineluctable*	64
Spring is a spider	65
One way of looking at a stone	66
Magus	67
Competitions & Poems Previously Published	69
Notes	71
Acknowledgements	72
Biography	75

* See Notes at the end of the book for further information about form and vocabulary.

November

No longer afternoon,
nor yet dusk.
The sun, besieged by cloud,
hunkers down
behind the parapet
of Witcombe Wood,
casting a chill shadow
across fields tussocked
with straggly stems of wheat
long harvested.

Yet still, on Birdlip, trees
are turned to burnished bronze,
Crickley's cliff
angel-ed in evening light.

Two pheasant scutter for cover
across the unploughed furrows,
heads held high
in implausible dignity.
In plash and soss,
the day, the year is dying.

Shadow now too
upon the reservoir,
part mirror,
part black-barred
with little waves.
Twice a great fish, leaping, slaps
the surface and is gone.

Coot cry sharp accusations
at the gathering dark.

There is a sadness
on the face of the water
as one struck suddenly lonely
in the company of friends.

Lineover Wood

a 'reduction' poem

These woods of oak and ash and lime
are blessed with ferns and Roman snails
and, in their June glory, orchids –
Pyramidal, Common Spotted, Butterfly –
dappled sun and leaves against the sky.

The secrets of this land are mine
no less than his who, staring into Wales,
stood Saxon heir to what lies hid
here amid the trees, the deep refrain
of Gloucestershire, now heard again.

In Witcombe Wood

Come with me in May to Witcombe Wood,
when ramsons are all I sense and see.

Or, in March, when the heart stops
at a far-off blaze of almost alien red
showing that once again elf caps
have staged their brief epiphany.

Or, at other times, look down
between the boles of trees
to the waters of the reservoir below,
imagining the sharp imperatives of coot,
two courting grebe
like stiff-necked barristers bewigged,
serene insouciance of swans.

Mussel shell

At the water's edge,
a mud-encrusted shell
shaped like some steep-sided
undulation of the age-worn Downs,
contours marked upon it
as on a survey map in raised relief,
understated, satisfactory.

Contrast
the iridescence,
the empyrean grace
of pure nacre,
an affirmation seen only
when the mollusc's dead.

May the drab integument
of my own heart
one day prove to hide
such sure radiance,
such subtlety.

Shells

Here in this handful
are a hundred shells.
As each wave breaks
upon this short stretch of shore,
it casts the fleeting purposes
of countless former limpet lives
one upon another,
grinding shy ribbed symmetries
imperceptibly to sand.

Drought

That summer
of rain and low cloud
the words came easily,
pattering on roof-tiles,
channelled chortling
and guggling into gutters
and downpipes,
barrels brimming
with an abundance of hope.
Freshets trickling, purling
in celebration
of Perperuna, of Dudulya.
Reservoirs swelling,
dimpled with fat drops,
ripple-ringed with rising fish,
sluices exuberant
as a mountain spate
at snow-melt in spring.

So soon, sluice-dry September.
Drought left me stranded,
a diving-beetle on its back,
feathered legs no longer flailing.

Damp humours
i.m. Job Yate (1594–1668), Rector of Rodmarton

If you would have this book [??] be sure to aire it att the fire or in the sunne three or foure times a year or it will grow dankish and rott, therefore looke to it. It will not be amiss also when you find it dankish to wipe over the leaves with a dry woollen cloath. This place is very much subject to dankishness. Therefore I say looke to it. inscribed by the Revd Job Yate in the Parish Register of Rodmarton (then called Rodmerton), Gloucestershire, which is in fact one of the 'driest' parishes in the county, having no stream, pond or lake within its bounds. In the Middle Ages, a community of monks deserted the area because of the lack of water.

A volume worthy of its purpose, weighty
and foursquare, its pages of the finest vellum –
enough of them, should mankind last so long,
for four centuries of such recording – bound
in the supple skins of two yearling calves.
A book in which I write what piques my fancy
of curious happenings here in the stonebrash
acres, traversed by ancient paths, that men call
Rodmerton – in which I chronicle the names
of the baptised, of persons joined in wedlock,
of those whose bodies moulder in the sacred ground,
their souls (if it please God) fled to a better place.

I have done what a pastor can to instill
a sense of history in my flock. But they
do not listen. Their quotidian heads think
only of Ship Money, of the burden
of the parish rates that go to feed the poor.

They do not feel the fenny fingers of the damp.
When I complain of it, they laugh at me
behind my back. I sense it everywhere,
dripping stealthily at night, clammy
on my waking brow. And not only on these
drear February days when spring seems
to have decamped leaving its traces
only in a straggle of catkins. No matter
the parish boasts no brook within its bounds:
these humours are palpable in the stones
of the old church, sweat from the young elms I planted
on the green, seep from my own dwelling's beams.

So to those who will follow me I have inscribed
herein some earnest words, admonishing them
to beware this dankishness, to let the book
breathe in the morning sun, to wipe the pages
carefully with a soft cloth. May they take heed!

Peter Grimes

Scarcely a breeze.

An unremitting sky broods,
brow cloud-furrowed,
pent heavy with suspense.

Intransigent, the sea
heaves and swells,
plucking like a petulant child
at the skirts of the shore.
Even the gulls are fled inland.

Too soon
Caliban will rage and howl
in thrashing anguish
for his lost Miranda.

No boat will venture out today.

After the rain

Today,
after long days
of heavy rain,
heaven has opened
a blue eye
on a world stirring
from sleep, buds
on brink of breaking.

The lane is flooded.
There before me
an image of the sky
unruffled by merest
breath of wind,
depth echoing depth,
a hall of mirrors
receding to
infinity.

In the flooded lane

this breathless afternoon
it is hard to tell
which is water, which is sky.

Two worlds answer each other
in the same timeless syllables,
past and future
melded imperceptibly in now.

In winter

Staghorn coral of an antlered oak.
Rooks drift, shadowed angel-fish
in silhouette against
a martyred evening sky.

Wind wailing and wauling in the eaves,
as night rain, importunate as a bailiff,
peppers the window-panes
in a frenzy of frustrated spite.

Rare days of icicle and sparkling snow,
reminders that all clichés once
were new.

Camera obscura of high-hedged flooded lane
on some halcyon day in March, reflecting
bare branches on the brink of leaf-break
in a fathomless empyrean
of eggshell blue.

The exuberance of moss,
when all around is dun and wan,
proclaiming that the one truth is green.

Branches

Bare, brave against a cloudless sky,
fallen, yet vibrant with a majesty of moss,
lichened gallery of abstract art,
snow-laden in Dog Lane.

Spider threads

Until that moment,
to us invisible.
But in an instant,
picked out by the precise angle
of a westering November sun,
from tussock to tussock
another and another
wherever the eye rested
over a hillside
now scintillant, bewitched –
the unconscious horizontal artistry
of uncountable tiny creatures,
defying both photograph
and metaphor.

Keys to a kingdom

Hedgerows, verges, borders, paths,
wastelands where little else will grow –
all fertile ground for me,
awaiting my airborne colonists,
a vegetable *lebensraum*.

Overnight, it seems,
my bud-tipped spears
appear, defying
any mere human hand
to root them out.

My winged progeny
scattered to the winds,
how is it that
I do not rule the world?

Last fruit

The gage that once
was gorged with plums
is dying. Low down,
a straggle of faded leaves.
The topmost branches gaunt
and bare. Plague-marks
of fungus blister the trunk. Ivy
begins its inexorable
smothering rise.
                    Yet,
at head height, a jewel
filled with the autumn sun –
a single tear of amber
distils the light, flames
with inner fire.

Ivy

I am Kissos,
nymph possessed of Furies
incarnate in the god of wine.
I danced ecstatic
into the arms of death,
rose again as plant
the solstice cannot kill,
my late flowers
drowsy with the obsequies
of drunken bees.

I am the spirit of resurrection
in a woman's guise,
my gemstone
yellow serpentine,
tendrils coiling supple as a snake,
hederal houri twining sinuous limbs
around all upstanding things,
throwing a Circe's cloak
about the spellbound
masculinity of oak and ash.

I am she who cast a green shadow
upon the face of Osiris,
imprinted the image of my leaves
on the sleek bodies
of eunuch priests of Cybele and Attis,
circled the frenzied heads of maenads
calf-drunk on hederine,

marked with my sacred spiral
the phallic fingerposts
of mediaeval inns.

I am bindwood and lovestone.
My sympathetic magic,
infusion of leaf or corymb,
relieves the drunkard's
throbbing brow,
soothes sun-bruised skin
with essence of the moon,
salves intimate inflammations,
quinine to fevers
of the whispering eye.

I am she the Fathers
sought to extirpate
from churches, fearful
of the potency
of old gods. I laughed
at them, smothering towers
and porches, running rampant
over graves
of young girls who died
of disappointed love.

Halcyon wars

Painter's palette
of bright oils
sheen shadowed,
bravura on a branch,
potentiality of power –
fish fearsome,
poised for dive
or arrow flight.

Now appears
a river rival,
equally ablaze,
desperate,
mate-less,
bent on
bride-rights,
hazards all
for scope
to procreate.

Such feathered
ferocity,
beak to beak,
bone to bone,
flailing,
tumbling
flightless
down, down
to do
or drown.

Splash
of close-bound
bodies,
thrashing,
inseparable
to death.
Commotion
brings bankside
predator
to prey.
Mink mouthful.
Mute.

Sparrowhawk

Today,
a hawk came briefly to me,
brushed me with her wing.

I knew nothing of her coming,
nor why she came.

Turned at her touch
to see her
flying from me, low and fast.

Were I to wait a lifetime
standing where I stood,
I doubt I'd ever feel again
those feathers stroke my arm.
But I'd surely face the other way
and hope to see her come.

Swifts

bouts rimés

They sleep, these aerial acrobats,
while on the wing. I have no doubt they dream
of speed. Most birds rejoice in song. Swifts scream
their elation. God's carefree cosmocrats,
they fling their untamed *requiescats*
in celeritate in an eye-beam
and are gone. In that instant, they redeem
all melody they lack.
                              Monochromats
see only black and white, more than somewhat
deprived of tone. Yet sound and 'sight accrew
to lure' even for them when swifts' untold
exhilaration and sheer speed besot
the senses, outshine all birds of brighter hue,
their scimitar black more gold than gold.

Aerobatics

Folk flock to Fairford,
who might watch for free
the swifts' display
about the Abbey's towers,
affirming the moment
with each exultant cry.

The Devil's birds they call them.
If that is the sound of hell,
what must heaven's be?

The Magpie with a broken wing

Once, when I could fly,
I'd perch in the tree-tops
sending you wild
with my insistent death-cackle,
cling crazily
to the peanut-feeder
keeping all other birds at bay.
I was a spoiler and no mistake –
and took delight in it.

But then I took
one chance too many in the lane,
pecking at some gruesome morsel
for a breath too long.

The car caught me a glancing blow,
shattered my wing.

Life changed.
Now getting my meals
is no picnic. I've had to learn
to get to those tree-tops
in a series of hops
from bough to bough, to bounce
like a bobbing ball across the lawn.

But here's the surprising thing.

You, who once loathed me
and my irritating ways,
now rejoice to see I've made
another day, admire my resilience,
wish that you could see me well.

Bumbarrel Valentine

Sri-sri sri-sri.

You've arrived,
you and the gang
in a joyful scrum
of pygmy picnickers.

Other birds scatter before me,
finches, dunnocks, blackbirds,
great tits, hightailing it
for the hedge. Some
make scarce even at a hint
of movement at a window –
woodpeckers with a startled cry,
seeming to part the air like swimmers
swimming butterfly, rooks heaving
their pantalooned bulk aloft, Lancasters
bound for some avian Möhne Dam,
magpies bunny-hopping into flight
to perch, tails flicking
in irritation, in the nearest tree.

Yet you –
everything that you are
little bigger than a thumb
cocooned in feathers –
you show no fear,
but wait expectant
as I put out food.

Last week, I saw you
snap up an eager morsel,
not in your beak, but with the toes
of a diminutive foot, flit
to a twig not three feet
from me, pause perplexed
balanced on one leg,
then delicately present
foot to beak, food to mouth,
like a left-handed lady
of impeccable refinement
in a café eating cake.

Heron

Malevolent prelate,
gaunt on a branch
of the dead oak,
shoulders hunched,
long legs a mirror
of austerity.

Then, in the shallows,
wrapt attention
of an unerring eye,
beak poised to strike
with speargun finality.

Yet, you fly
with the unhurried languor
of a slowly shaken rug.

Welcome home

Grim walking.
Cloud down over the hills,
the odd spit of spiteful rain,
a bully-boy wind buffeting
my face, the now familiar
tightening of the chest
that robs progress
of all pleasure.

Twenty minutes, no more,
but it seems an ice-age
before I trudge like Oates
up the last slope
to my front door.

Yet, as I rummage for my keys,
it is there again,
not three feet away,
head cocked, blush-pink toes
gripping the gate-top,
an expectant eye
regarding me without fear –
almost, it seems, a friend.

The last passenger pigeon
died Cincinnati Zoo, 1 September 1914

August.

And, in my dream,
a shadow, vast as history,
is moving upon the earth.
The sky pulsates
with the multitude
of my forgotten kin,
their numbers multiplying
as they wing
blindly into the past.

Waking,
I strut,
earthbound
and alone.

Far to the east,
other guns stand ready to repeat
the immemorial folly.

Tomorrow,
for me,
they will finally be still.

Birds
bouts rimés

Birds – the sight of them, the sound – delight where
mirth and all else we craft falls short. And why?
Words are mere perturbations of the air.
Earth, if set stark beneath a bird-less sky,
nightmare that would bring us to the brink.
Drink in the song of nightingale, lintwhite
whitethroat, wren! While birds be still with us, drink!
Brink indeed. To lose them would be as night –
sky would take on the opacity of earth,
air the empty pretensions of our words.
Why do we waste ourselves in pointless mirth
where we have for the taking – joy in birds?

Pecking orders
syllabics

You may have noticed
how tits at the feeders
will grab a morsel and scarper,
while finches just guzzle.

In winter, redpolls
vie with the goldfinches
for the best of the nyger-seed
and usually win.

Bullfinches seldom
allow other species
to share their space at the seed-tray,
for all there is plenty.

Often they see off
other bullfinches too,
females ousting much stouter males.
Yet both yield to their young.

But cock of the roost
with which none will tangle
is the great spotted woodpecker
and that razor-sharp beak.

In all the text-books,
the robin's a byword
for aggressive behaviour
to most other small birds.

Yet in my garden,
though dunnocks are fair game,
my pusillanimous namesake
defers to a blue tit.

Old friend

You've seldom had
a good press, old friend,
not at least on these shores.

In Chaucer's day, the epitome
of cowardice – and comic cowardice at that.

Then you became
the witch's accomplice, paradigm
of unloveliness – even, absurdly,
censured for slime.

Mr Grahame at least
endowed you with some
redeeming traits. Yet,
the enduring picture
is of Trump-like vainglory.

And to Larkin,
however much an old familiar,
you were still the image
of the daily grind.

Small comfort perhaps
that, when I encounter you,
whether your warty self,
defiant eyes, jutting Churchillian chin,
lumbering
like some muscle-bound heavy
slowly into view

or, of a wet evening in March,
your progeny braving
the dank Sahara of Dark Lane,

I count myself blessed.

Grass snake

I saw, I think, its absence
only – as it were, the motion
of the air it had displaced,
a soft settling
of mown grass.

And there
where it had lain,
delicate, diaphanous,
sloughed like an evening glove,
like a silk stocking
from some languid lady's leg,
the perfect image
of its former self.

Sloth

Deliberate as a mushroom's growth,
I plot my ponderous
path from branch
to branch, the time-lapsed
articulation of my limbs
mimics the stick insect,
my grasp as the chameleon's,
and as slow.

Be not deceived:
my passions race
quick as the chameleon's
tongue, swifter than the jaguar's
leap, fervent
as piranhas' frenzy.

Monkey sanctuary

They come in droves to giggle
and gawp, to ooh and aah, to take
predictable selfies
with an obliging ape.
Their tenners fund
our enterprise – we cannot say
them nay.   Yet, I wonder –
the macaques, the capuchins,
the tamarins, the langurs,
the lemurs and the drills,
do they wonder in their turn

'Who is the monkey here?'

Pigs

Few things more *satisfying* than a pig,
unless it be two or three.
The unhurried corpulence,
the absorption in soaking up
sun, scrumping
for succulent roots, the blithe
abandonment of mud –
the moment of now.

Each time I pass,
I scan the threatened field
fearful I have seen the last
of that august rotundity.
And, if they are not
hidden, indolent,
in their makeshift styes,
cry 'PIGS!'
to a startled sky.

In a small way

Lift a stone, observe
the world beneath, absorb
the details one by one
as the eye adjusts
to an alien scale.

A woodlouse coiled
in overlapping splints,
Lilliputian armadillo.
A beetle, oil-spill black, legs spread
and poised for flight. Two slugs
camouflaged against pale
slug-ochre soil. Worms
anaemic from the lack of light.
A hair's-breadth centipede,
new hatched, finding a crack
where surely no crack could be,
is sucked in, slick
as a vacuum flex.
A spider's eggs
cocooned in silk.

And there above,
on a ripening apple, a nodule
morphs into a minute snail
glued immobile
on the massive fruit.

A questing blue tit –
behemoth vast
beyond imagining.

Cornish miracle

All this dapple day,
it has been drowse
and dream. Still
as the soft breath
of a dozing child. Cirrus clouds,
a reverie above, curled
comfortable as cats. Hypnotic
bubblings from the iridescent
throats of doves. The little sounds
of summer and of sleep.

Then in the sunbright
of an August afternoon,
suddenly
it is snowing –
fat flakes drifting, jinking,
backlit, it seems, as if
by Christmas lights,
flickers of pink and mustard,
hints of green.

Snowing butterflies.

In a time of prayer

'Our Father, which art . . .'

Chairs not pews. No kneelers here,
so we pray, heads
bowed like Methodists
and sitting.

'. . . our trespasses . . .'

I gaze down
at the floor beneath my feet.
There, in a shallow divot
in the ancient stone
is . . . well, I can't tell what it is.
A seed perhaps
from last summer's grass?
A piece of grit?

'Lead us not . . .'

Lozenge shaped, a fraction of
a fraction of an inch.
Or is it even . . . ?
Yes, indeed it is.
For, at that moment,
two minute antennae start
to test the air. It moves
a smidgin, as if
uncertain where to go or when,
shrinks back, then moves again.

'. . . the power and the glory . . .'

And now it's off. I infer
twin maniples
of unseen legs working
in tandem to carry it
across the barren steppe
and out of sight behind
the Everest
of my neighbour's shoe.

'Amen.'

Glass

A bluebottle skitters and bumps across the pane
frustrate at the obdurate transparency of glass,
by chance flies sideways to where a light's ajar,
finds, defenestrate, unfettered freedom in the air.

Has it come to this?

I should be rejoicing
in the evening light,
in the shadows encroaching
on the hedge-bound lane,
in breeze-born ripples
that stroke the surface of the lake
dying to a molten image
of the setting sun.

I should be savouring
the scent of lavender,
the hint of wood smoke
on the tranquil air.

I should be listening
to the whisper of the leaves.
to the blackbird's
darkling *au revoir* . . .
to the soft rhythm
of my fitful heart.

But no.

There is another
Twitter thread to read,
another Facebook posting,
another Quordle challenge
to complete before
the nightly ritual
of a Would I Lie To You? repeat.

The pool

The pool
she had known at all seasons:
reed mace a bearskinned guard;
marsh marigolds and crowfoot;
chain-mailed with duck-weed;
murky and bare in winter
or crusted and crazed with ice.

There had been dragonflies
to watch on summer afternoons
hawkers, darters, demoiselles,
coruscant jump jets,
hovering, then sling-shot quick.
In the still air, she could hear
the urgent, soft, clicking
of translucent wings.

And delicate damselflies,
banded blue and black,
clasped to grass stems
or to pungent agrimony.

Pond-skaters, whirligigs.

Once, she had caught,
as she approached,
a small sound
as if of a frog diving,
but had seen,
not a frog,
but the head and neck

of a miniature monster
cauled green in weed
break the surface
for a frantic second
before the depths reclaimed it.

In March, the mating toads
filled her ears
with the multitude
of their low release calls.
She watched in awe
the tangle of ungainly bodies
locked in the imperative
of the amplexus.

Even on monochrome days
before spring, there were chats
clinging to the tops of swaying reeds,
their mild alarms
like the clack of billiard balls.

* * *

Now, after the years of drought,
where the pool once was,
nothing but mace
and bitter agrimony.

Dark Lane

The name, I'm sure I've read,
indicates an ancient track,
trodden for centuries
by man and beast.

In this case –
or so my late aunt alleged –
once the main highway,
hard to credit though it is,
from periwigged Cheltenham
to the kindred pleasure grounds
of Bath.

No tarmac then, of course.
But no doubt, as now,
pot-holes, flowing streams
of water off the hill,
great swathes of mud,
a liberal supplement
of equine dung.

A metaphor, it seems,
for the dark lane of my life.

Yet, then as now,
from time to time lit up
by glimpse of puttock
proud on post or branch,
of bumbarrel, ouzel, bull spink,
of Joe Bent,
of other shy survivors of the wild –
badger, roe deer, foxes, toads.

Dee

Where sea becomes river, river
sea, not even the wind can tell.

There is a line far out
where a paler grey becomes
abruptly dark,
but, month on month
between Wirral and Wales,
year on year
as far as Flint,
the moon-dazed tide
drains, floods, drains
the mudflats, melding
land with ocean,
salt with fresh.

Out on the estuary
within an oarspull of the Little Eye
a small breath of birds
wheels in a close-shifting
convex cloud
as a magnet draws iron filings
on paper from beneath,
and is lost to sight.

Here on Red Rocks Marsh
a long fallen tree
bleached white,
the sea's writhings locked in wood,

and smart as humbugs
the lemon and chocolate whorls
of countless snails.

A single lark
chimneys upward
singing,
heedless,
to the battling wind.

Beeching

Here,
I stood, waving
a little flag
to the King
as he trundled by
in state.

Here,
one might have imagined
Poirot, umbrella
neatly furled,
alighting to confound
some murderous scion
of the sleepy shires.

Here,
one unsuspecting day –
it was the year of Suez, of tanks
in Budapest – progress
arrived, disguised
as the latest thing
in one-horse, two-coach
diesel cars.

In them, we rattled up the line
to Banbury, past
fields of dreaming cows, past
halts – Radclive, Water Stratford,
Fulwell, Farthinghoe – where
no one ever seemed to halt,

crossing and recrossing
the meandering Ouse.

Now,
no posters flaunting
wholesome girls
on Filey beach, no waiting churns,
no crates of day-old
hatchling chicks, no prudent
buckets filled with builder's sand,
no porter's bike leant
casually against a wall.

The whole creation's
gone, not even a path
to show where once
the railway ran.

Brambles, buddleia
and crumpled cans.

Night walk at Stowe

An antidote to loss,
this frozen moon,
dwarfing the constellations,
casts vast shadows
on the tomb-blanched grass.

Trees, grave as senators,
bear silent witness
to my grief. Sheep,
insubstantial ghosts,
bleating softly, make way
for this unlikely
night-time stranger.

Away to my right, the glint
of Eleven-Acre Lake.
A single sharp cry.
The wakeful coot
is still again.

I pass the dome
of Vanburgh's Rotunda,
its gilt Venus centuries gone,
and on down Gurnet's Walk,
between the lakes, turn east,
skirt the Pebble Alcove,
its intricate heraldry
invisible at night.

And there before me
the Temple of Friendship,
now a ruin swathed
in rampant ivy,
haunted monument
to the passing
of what once seemed
immortal.

Anchor Island
Dusky Sound, Fiordland, New Zealand

No effort here to feel
what the world once was
without us, what we have lost
by simply being.

          Here,
a timeless benign conspiracy
of trees – tawhai, rata,
totara, rimu – of mosses
in every cast of green,
of sculpted ferns,
of liverworts.

          Here
the silence echoes
to the eerie cries of birds –
tui, saddleback, mohua,
even the bittern boom
of kakapo.

Now, all visitors must undergo
a cleansing, may arrive
only by air, must submit
to exhaustive rules
and questioning, lest disease
or alien predators invade.

Yet it is not the seeds,
the larvae, the excreta
and the insect eggs
that truly threaten paradise.

For all our precautions, for all
our well-meaning care,
it is ourselves.

Earth

So we have named our world,
the soil that sustains us.
Earth is where the heart is,
first to last.

Yet, for us, there is more –
the whisper of a gentle breeze
through aspen leaves,
dancing water in a rivulet,
waves withdrawing
on some distant shore,
clouds in a breathless sky,
the setting sun.

How must it seem
to a springtail,
for which earth is truly all?
No sea, no sky –
unless Armageddon strikes,
no light, no wind, no fire.

Schrödinger's mole

Moles and philosophers seldom mix.
For the philosophy of moles is
not to *think* about much, beyond food
and, once in a twelvemonth, the odd bout
of talpine sex. Even spring-cleaning
tends to get short shrift. Yet one could say
that a philosopher's life is quite like
that of a mole – a nose for what is
important and only that, working
diligently in the dark to make
sense of a tunnel, tossing aside
the irrelevant, the contrary,
irreverently depositing
molehills on our neat, complacent lawns.

The Wild Hunt

Not a single star
relieves the mantle of the night.
The world sleeps
as if dead.
Silence save for the whisper
of the falling snow.

I cannot see them, but,
on all sides, the trees, I know,
march into an endless future,
an endless past.
Then, far off, a wolf
howls.

And it begins.

Primaeval

Bones and more bones –
aurochs, bison, deer.
The steady drip of moisture.
Walls clammy and glistening
with blind
and crawling things.
The torch gutters
and goes out.

Darkness and no fire.
Darkness and my own self.

Pax Romana

Sandalled feet
slapping on well-tamped stones,
rhythmic swish of skirts, soft
clink of armour, sometimes
a barked command.

It is summer.

On either side, trees
march to the horizon,
green on green. Ahead,
the road, a purposeful,
a sober sameness,
does obeisance to neither
hill nor stream.
No wayward English drunkard
traced its course.

The cohort stamps on
in smart formation
to the next encampment,
nexused and neat as a crossword,
like the last.

Yet, among the trees,
small creatures follow
their ancestral ways,
dip and jink
around bole and boulder,
between rock and root.

They too have purposes.
They too live out their lives.

King Lear on Crickley Hill

Apparition from a world
of myth
or make-believe.
One might almost see
some Mordred figure
come to claim
his crooked throne,
stepping, in the blink
of a sun-dazed eye,
out from among trees
where, surely, no man
had been a trice before.
Or Lear dispossessed and
shadowed only by the Fool,
bearing, a negligent
and laggardly lictor,
a sorry clutch of
loosely gathered sticks.

Eutopia

Sometimes, while the stars are sleeping,
I take the evening by the arm,
seldom hear the foxgloves weeping,
spell-bound by the thrush's psalm.
From time to time, a scent arises
as if of candles newly lit.
Its all-embracing power disguises
the reek of rotting from the pit.
Just think of all the nightmare visions
some people take for Shangri-La.
Their very act of faith imprisons
the minds that hanker for a star.
There would seem sense in simply turning
back to what we love the most.
But, as a rule, a boat's for burning,
so seek the solace of the coast.

The ineluctable
bouts rimés

He who, exiled to an unknown wood,
while wandering, has understood
the ferment of the storm-lashed fir,
how autumn gales administer
the verdict of a hunter's moon
that spring's resolve must falter soon –
sees also how the unforeseen
leaves footprints where the past has been,
how these are merely days of grace
before the Hippocratic face.

He who despite it all forgives
the world's enormity outlives
the intake of that final breath,
outlives the certainty of death.

Spring is a spider

motionless at the centre of a web,
eight legs outstretched.
At the extremity of each leg,
a single drop of dew
reflecting the early sunlight,
reflecting a mood, coruscant
with the promise of rebirth.

Spring is a drop of dew
trembling by the seventh segment
of a spider's leg.
As the day lengthens,
it diminishes, to leave
only the thread of silk
on which it once rested,
all light extinguished.

One way of looking at a stone

No one has seen the centre of this stone.
No one has heard the rain falling
on piano keys at the edge of dusk.
This the thrush knows,
the thrush whose head is held aslant
to listen for the turning of the worm,
a sound softer than the cat's footfall
on new-mown turf –
as sacred as the centre of this stone.

Magus

He senses a miracle in the sculpted bark of cedars,
    an absence in the flight of gulls,
remembers what the mole remembers
    on soft nights under the moon,
sees a brother in the white-nosed rabbit,
    a master in the slow urgency of snails.

His wisdom is manifest in the silent wings of owls.

He fears the sun and the moon equally,
yet dreads still more the brooding of clouds
    on poplar leaves in spring.

On the lake, amid the coot-stepped lilies,
    his shadow drowns.

Competitions & Poems Previously Published

'November' won the Gloucestershire Prize in the Buzzwords Poetry Competition, 2015.

'Swifts' was one of three runners-up in the *Oldie* bouts rimés competition, 2019.

'Grass snake' was runner-up for the Gloucestershire Prize in the Buzzwords Poetry Competition, 2018.

'Dee' was one of five commended poems in the Buzzwords Poetry Competition, 2019.

'Beeching' came second in the Buzzwords Poetry Competition, 2018.

'Schrödinger's mole' was Highly Commended in the *Cannon's Mouth* Sonnet or Not competition in 2018.

* * *

'Drought', 'In the flooded lane' and 'Earth' were published in the Cheltenham Poetry Society anthology *The Elements* in 2022.

'Spider threads' was published in issue 040 of T*he Dawntreader*, autumn 2017.

'Cornish miracle' was published in issue 043 of *The Dawntreader*, summer 2018.

Notes

Syllabic poetry is a form of verse where the metre is determined solely by the number of syllables per line, ignoring the stress placed on any individual syllable, i.e., each line has a set number of syllables, regardless of how they are emphasized when spoken.

A **reduction poem**, which may rhyme, but does not have to, has two five-line stanzas, in which a portion of one word from every line of the first stanza appears in the corresponding line of the second.

A *bouts rimés* poem is one composed from a set of predetermined rhyme-words, as part of a competition or less formal challenge, the most famous example being Shelley's 'Ozymandias'. The rhyme-words are sometimes taken from an existing poem.

All three *bouts rimés* poems in the book were entries for competitions in the *Oldie*. The rhyme words given for 'Swifts' were taken from 'Nebuchadnezzar's Dream' by Keats, not perhaps one of his masterpieces. Those for 'Birds' were taken from 'The Tewkesbury Road' by John Masefield and those for 'The ineluctable' from 'Death lies in wait for you, you wild thing in the wood', also by John Masefield.

Regional bird names ('Birds', 'Bumbarrel Valentine', 'Dark Lane'): lintwhite – linnet; bumbarrel – long-tailed tit; puttock – red kite or (as here) buzzard; ouzel – blackbird; bull spink – bullfinch; Joe Bent – great tit.

Perperuna and **Dudulya** (Drought) – rain goddesses in Slavic mythology.

Acknowledgements

My writing owes a great deal to a great many people who grace the fertile local poetry scene in Gloucestershire and to quite a few from further afield. To try to name them all would not only result in a very long list indeed, but I'd also run the risk of inadvertently (and hurtfully) overlooking someone who should be included. So I shall have to be very selective in naming names, though many others are implied by the various groups referred to.

My sincere thanks go:

to all fellow members, over the years, of the Writing Group of the Cheltenham Poetry Society;

to Angela France, onlie begetter of Buzzwords, and all those who have led workshops I have attended there;

to David Ashbee and all those who have read and played at Holub;

to Roger Turner, Sharon Larkin and all others who have led CPS workshops, especially at CPS Away Days;

to Peter Wyton, who introduced me to all these groups and has read with me several times at Cheltenham Poetry Festival events;

to Peter, Kathy Alderman, Frankie & Geoff March and Gill Garrett, fellow members of the Cheltenham Poetry Festival Players;

to all those who have led workshops I have attended at, or sponsored by, the Cheltenham Poetry Festival, especially David Clarke, Alicia Stubbersfield and Rhian Edwards;

to Jennie Farley, Su Billington and their helpers for so many wonderful evenings at New Bohemians in Charlton Kings;

to Alison Brackenbury and Ross Cogan, who, among other kindnesses, (with Angela, Peter and Anna) so generously reviewed my previous collection *DaDa & the Dark Lady*;

to Anna Saunders for her tireless work on the Cheltenham Poetry Festival and for her inspirational workshops at Suffolk Anthology and The Sober Parrot and to all those who attended them and other informal sessions led by Anna.

Biography

Robin Gilbert was born in Oxford a few days after the end of the Second World War. He wrote his first poem, over which a veil is discreetly drawn, at the age of five. In his early years, he was privileged during school holidays to have the run of the grounds at Stowe, where his father taught. He himself was educated at preparatory schools, Winchester House and Orwell Park, and at Tonbridge, before going up to Oxford, where he read Greats at Balliol. After graduation, he taught for two terms at Pocklington School near York as the (instructive) price for spending much of the summer in Italy. There followed three happy, if academically not very productive, years back at Balliol researching in Republican Roman history. Needing the means of financial support, he then joined the Government Communications Headquarters (GCHQ) in Cheltenham, where he worked for thirty-four years, retiring in January 2006. Not long after retirement, he began to attend meetings of Buzzwords, the Cheltenham Poetry Society and Holub, which have all been invaluable sources of inspiration and encouragement for his writing. From 2013 to 2019, he was co-director of the Cheltenham Poetry Festival. Apart from a three-year posting overseas, he has lived, since 1972, in Bentham, beneath Crickley Hill, within the area of the 'Wide Valley', which has provided the material for many of the poems in this book.